IT'S ALL ONLY TEMPORARY

Memories of a Dublin Childhood in the 1950s and 60s

Margaret Hayward

Copyright © 2025 by Margaret Hayward

All rights reserved. No part of this book may be reproduced, stored in a retrieval system, or transmitted in any form or by any means, electronic, mechanical, photocopying, recording, or otherwise, without the prior written permission of the author or publisher, except for brief quotations used in reviews or scholarly works.

Table of Contents

A Temporary Man 1

Baby Blues 5

Running Home to Booterstown 7

Saturdays 13

Nuclear War 17

The Secret 19

A Cowboy and a Dog called Trigger 21

Dave The Prince of Tides 25

The Honeymoon 31

A Woman, Most Royal 35

Mrs Glaudeman 41

Adventure in India 45

The Town Hall 51

Winnie 55

The Wife of Bath 59

A Grave Affaire 63

Queen of Supplements 67

The Flask People 69

A short one act play 73

A Tribute To Dublin 77

A Temporary Man

My Father was temporary man. He had a temporary job in the council, painting the seats on the seafront in the Summer and such like. But winters found him idle so, he did the jobs round the house, and garden, which needed doing. In a temporary fashion of course.! He put up shelves and pelmets, and hung pictures with a temporary nail. My Mother would look at the shaky shelves with a critical eye and say," that looks as if it's going to fall down." He'd say '''ah its only temporary ''Sure it will be grand''. So, we had a house of falling shelves and pictures hanging from shaky nails.

We children were wise to the dangers; we walked sideways up the stairs avoiding the flying ducks hanging on temporary nails ready to fly off. We never walked under the hanging shelves or under the pictures hanging perilously on the wall. But of course, not everyone knew of the dangers. One Easter when the priest called for the Easter Dues he sat on the chair with the temporary leg, and fell to the ground. My poor Mother was mortified. When the priest hastily left, my father said grinning` `he got his Easter dues all right´ ´We kids laughed uproariously, as we were quite a dysfunctional family really.

IT'S ALL ONLY TEMPORARY

My Mother worried a lot, this was because my father didn't worry at all, so she felt she had to worry on his behalf. She worried about bills, she worried about colds and flu, and damp clothes, and she worried about worrying. My Father didn't worry at all, he just went about his temporary jobs, with a hammer in his hand saying' 'sure it will be grand''.

He would take up hobbies temporarily, of course. One time he brought home hens. We would be having the life of Reilly he told us, with our fresh eggs every day. But the hens never stayed in the run, they sat on the windowsills pecking in the window at us, we had to close the curtains when we ate. They laid their eggs everywhere, apart from in the nest. We had a terrible job finding them. They ate all the grass and flowers; the garden was like a First World War trench, with mud everywhere. They woke us up in the morning, cocking and crowing. But when they began laying eggs without shells, that was the last straw," lack of grit, "my father said defending them. But my mother insisted they had to go. '' we will find a good home for them he said they'll be grand''. So, he did, a nice warm oven, at 350degrees.

After the hen fiasco, he decided to read the Greek classics. Boxes of beautiful red leather-bound books started to arrive at the house. My Mother worried about the payment, but my father, assured her, he'd given a temporary payment. He built a temporary shelf for the books in the good room. The good room was really only for guests, but strangely enough we didn't have many guests visiting. The books stood grandly in their red and gold binding on the shelf. Just leaning slightly forward. I had a feeling Homer and Socrates were in for a big fall.

Sometime later he was offered a job painting the lighthouses. He loved it, as he was away a lot. As I'm sure he wished at time, that we kids were temporary as well, with our ever-growing feet that needed shoes and our ever-growing appetites. But my mother soon put a stop to his happiness and ordered him home. So really his time at the lighthouse was temporary as well. But he had written a poem while he was there so it wasn't in vain. Much to our embarrassment he regaled everyone with the poem, "OH the mist, the mist that kissed, the hill of hungry hill' 'If we felt brave enough to ask any of our friends in, we would warn him "not the poem daddy please.

But the most embarrassing of all was when he got the new false teeth. He was always a bit of a grinner, but with the new teeth, he grinned all the time, He loved those teeth, he thought they were gorgeous. I thought he looked like the Cheshire cat in Alice in wonderland. He grinned in the mirror; he grinned at the postman he grinned at the cats and dogs. Much to my sister's embarrassment who worked in the local shop, he grinned in at her, through the window frightening the life out of the customers.

One May Day without any warning, when he was building a porch at the house, he sat on a sun chair, and just passed away, no fuss, no doctors warning, no hospital visits. He just went. He was just 47. After the funeral, just looking at the temporary porch, I suddenly realised he was only with us temporary. I felt glad he never wasted his time worrying; he must have known he was only here for a short time.

The family was never really the same afterwards. The fun was gone out of it. I felt sure he was in heaven, in the temporary part, with his hammer, grinning, saying" sure, it will be all grand, don't worry". People say when you die, you're soon forgotten, but I disagree, as its now over 30 years since my temporary Father passed away. I still can see him in my mind's eye, grinning at me. I still remember him, especially when I'm hammering a temporary nail in the wall.

Baby Blues

While walking my dog in the park recently, I witnessed a young very pregnant woman letting her young child feel the movement in her vastly pregnant tummy, and tell her about her little sister. The little girl looked happy, and looked on in wonder at the movement in her mom's tummy. I watched and thought how very modern and very aware we have become, of young children's feelings. It brought me back nearly fifty years, to when I was five and the memory stays with me, and I still shiver. I then had a younger sister of four who I bossed around, and a toddler brother who I ignored, so I was very secure in my place in the family. One July morning just after my fifth birthday I awoke in my little bed to see, this figure in white in my room, well more cream really! WHERES MY MAMMY I said in fright? I noticed she had a big crucifix around her neck, but I wasn't sure what it was. *"Get up she told me your Mammy has had a new baby and your porridge is ready downstairs"*. We DON'T NEED ANOTHER BABY! I protested in all my five-year-old wisdom, but she didn't listen. *"Be a good girl"* she replied, *"your porridge is getting cold"*. I said, *"I DON'T EAT PORRIDGE< I HAVE ASTHMA!"* My sister and the other baby calmly did as they were told, and went downstairs to eat. I lay there and sulked. To this day I can still remember those feelings of shock, hurt, and surprise although I was too young g to put them into words. My Daddy was called and he came in and spoke to me softly about the new baby and the nice nun ("*Sisters of the Poor*)" who has come to look after us. I painstakingly tried to tell him" *Daddy we don't need another baby*", but he said," *she's here what can we do?*" I had a great idea then," *we can throw her out the window*". Of Course, they didn't do as I asked, but I then decided parents are not to be trusted, and was on my guard in case another baby arrived. A big sign I discovered was a big belly, if a mammy got a big belly, it was a sure sign. Another sign was a tin of talcum powder and two pins, that was a real give away! To powder a baby's bottom and pin a nappy on, I became a great detective on this baby business. My Mother told me years later, she felt lucky if she had the money to buy a few Greenfield nappies and two pins and talc. How things have changed when we look at the designer baby prams, and all the paraphilia of today. Then there was four! I wasn't aware of money and things like that, but when I went to the shops, I noticed the tight look on Mammy's mouth. When she asked the girl behind the counter for jam, the girl asked her, "*strawberry jam*", my mother would reply," *no they eat that, give me raspberry*!" My Mother was great at saving money she bought things we didn't like to make them last! I was always on my guard on another arrival, I didn't want that white figure with the cross appearing again, so I kept a good eye on her belly. I discussed it with my other little friends; we all tried to solve the puzzle. One pal said, "*it was something to do with a bird coming*," another one said, "*it was to do with cabbages*". We pondered the problem but didn't solve it. Lucky enough I was ten when the next baby arrived, but by then I was so sophisticated, when I saw the doctor arrive with the black bad, "*well I knew the baby was in the bag*".

Running Home to Booterstown

As a child I spent a lot of time with my Granny, Nanny, I called her. I went every Sunday, and I spent a week there, in summer in Booterstown. I loved going there. Nanny spoiled me. I was her namesake. We were close. So close, I didn't see her faults. Many people didn't like her as she spoke her mind. She once said to someone who was a little overweight, '" I was just looking at your big legs". ' Yes, you can see why she wasn't too popular with some people. I was the favorite, I also had a younger brother and sister, but she wasn't too keen on them. My little sister was quite small, and Nanny called her a midget. So much so, that a girl next door asked me to bring down the midget, she wanted to see her. I had to explain she wasn't a real midget, just quite small I was quite tall and thin, like Nanny, and she used to indicate because of that I would go far. She didn't hold with short people too much. When in fact it was the opposite, as my small sister who wasn't really a midget, did quite well in life. My young brother wasn't too popular either, as he touched things. Her Holland blind which was always pulled half down with the little tassel. Itchy little fingers ached to pull the tassel, and he did, and the blind shot up. After that he wasn't welcome any more. Which only left me I didn't mind too much, as I had her all to myself. And I wasn't too keen on the other two either. She was a wonderful cook and her lamb would melt in your mouth and potatoes like balls of flour. But shop keepers didn't dare give her anything but the best of everything, as with her sharp tongue she would soon bring it back to them. She never wrote shopping lists; just brought empty packets of the things she needed in her basket. She always wore a hairnet, and a navy housecoat to, save her clothes she said. I never did find out what she was saving her clothes for.

Every summer Nannie and I would write a list of things we would do on my week's holiday. The first was always a visit to her hairdresser, "we must get rid of that auld hair of yours' 'she would say. She didn't hold with long hair. Auld was a word she used a lot. " That auld wan" she would say as well as" how's your auld fellow". I always got the one and sixpenny cut, which had short back and sides and a little on top. She would have her hair set, and then plonk the hair net over it. My mother was always annoyed when I got back home with my short hair. Nanny wore drawers, she had them in pink, white, and red. They were ably named, as you could fit a lot of stuff in them. They reached her knees under which she wore stockings, this was pre tights days. The stockings were held up with elastic, garters they were called. The garters made red marks on her legs. They never seemed to go, even when she applied Ponds cold cream to them. Nanny swore by Ponds cold cream. When we went to the sea, she would paddle while I swam. But she always needed to take off her drawers. Being very modest, she would get me to hold the towel round her. I would always deliberately drop it. This always sent me into convulsions, at the sight of her fumbling with drawers and stockings to hide herself. ' 'Ur an awful auld cod" she would say. To this day I laugh at the memory.

Nanny had a friend, Ma Kelly, she would sometimes call for a chat, and they would sit by the fire, puffing at Woodbines and talk about who had died, they both looked up the obituaries every day. Nanny would say, "I'm just checking to see if I'm still here". It didn't seem to depress them at all in fact, they seemed to thrive on it. "I see auld Danny Doyle has passed on" Ma Kelly informs Nanny. "Him with the one leg"? asks Nanny." No, his brother "answers Ma Kelly, RIP. Nanny adds" he was an auld git to his wife; he would take a drink from a scabby leg". I used to listen to them, watching their netted heads nodding through the Woodbine smoke, and I learned a lot about life.

Nanny worked as a cleaner in the Protestant church, I loved to go and visit her there. You walked through a red velvet curtain to get to the pews. The pews had cushions to save your knees, unlike our Catholic hard board ones which numbed your knees. I remember thinking how we Catholics had to suffer with our poor knees, and no curtain to keep the draughts off us, not to mention having to go in a little box to tell your sins to a stranger. Nanny's Church smelt of polish and flowers unlike ours which smelt of incense and smelly feet. It had no statues of bleeding effigies either to give you the guilts either. When Nannie was there for 25 years, she had a mention in the Church magazine. I told her not to tell people, with all the snobbery of my youth, as I imagined I would become a writer, or a journalist. But life has a way of teaching us lessons.

The bonding began when I was a new-born. My mother had just come out of the hospital with me, and she was too nervous to bathe me so she put me in the pram and ran home to Booterstown to my Nanny. Like her mother before her, but I didn't know that story then, I was yet to find out. So, Nanny happily bathed me and from then on came specially to bath me, which formed the bond which was to last, till her death. When I was told she was seriously ill, I too ran home to Booterstown to see her. But I was too late; she had been taken to St Vincent's hospital. I quickly rushed there, hoping I would get to see her one last time. When I reached the ward, I immediately spotted the hairnet above the white sheet. There was a drip beside the bed, and an oxygen mask over her mouth. Between the mask and the hair net only her eyes were visible. I held her hand, her hands looked care worn with all the hard work she had done throughout her life. I don't think the Ponds cream had helped much. She looked at me and squeezed my hand. I told her to rest, and I would be back tomorrow. But sadly, she went in the night. I didn't know it then, but I was never to be spoiled again after she died.

Nanny hadn't wanted my mother to marry my father, because he was from Dun Laoghaire, and he never stopped grinning. Nannie didn't hold too much with people who grinned. And then on top of that his father was English and what was even worse, a British soldier. She called him auld Union Jack Harry. But, to her great disappointment, my mother did marry the grinning son of auld Union Jack Harry, and sometimes lived happily ever after. Maybe to compensate, they called the first baby after her. My father continued to grin at her, sometimes pulling her leg. He would say, ' "what do u think of the Royal visit to Africa" knowing well Nanny didn't hold too much with Royalty, "der always with dem blacks" she would reply, grim lipped. When his mother came to visit, Nanny was always aghast. At the way she dressed, " mutton dressed as lamb", she would say of the other granny. She didn't approve of her at all, marrying a British soldier and dying her hair blond. When she came to visit us, after a while she would get irritated with us, and then she would say, ' 'well I'm going home to Booterstown" Off she would go with an injured air about her.

As I began to grow up, I often wondered why there was no husband, and why Nanny was alone I asked her and she replied' 'grim lipped, he was a gun runner, he slept with his gun under his pillow" she would answer with disgust. I imagined a romantic figure, like Michael Collins, and wondered if the gun had gone off, and killed him in bed. Soon after my mother told me the fascinating story.

This happened around 1919 or 1920 just before the civil war. My Nanny seventeen-year-old girl who went to work at Boland's bakery, which still stands today near the Board Gais theatre. My Nanny who probably didn't wear a hairnet then, and was tall and slim met the young Paddy Fox then. I can see them in my mind's eye. He was from Gardener Street in the center of the city. She would have been very taken with him and his ideals of pro treaty, and of course his city ways. As I'm sure he was as taken with her from Booterstown, and she probably didn't speak her mind quite as much then as life tends to make us as we are. Soon after they married, and she went to live in Gardener Street as a young bride.

I really can't imagine it, as it was seldom spoken about. But I can suppose how it would have been for a young naive girl from Booterstown, to live in what was probably no more than a hovel as people then, lived in slums of Dublin. I'm sure it must have been tough for her, and she must have missed Booterstown greatly, the sea, and the quiet village type of life she was used too.

Well Nanny was made of stern stuff, and one day she took my mother who was then three, and a baby, and ran home to Booterstown. Just as my own Mother would do one day. This must have taken a lot of courage, as in those days single parents were unheard of. The only thing she'd had to leave one of the children there. This seems terrible by today's standards, but things were very different then, and we can't judge people by today's moral code. She found work cleaning, and she and the children settled back home very well. The problem was every so often, Paddy Fox would come looking for his wife and children. There was a field behind the house, and Nannie and her two children would hide in the ditch. My mothers first memories are been hid in a ditch and told to be quiet. After a while he stopped coming and life went on and my mother grew up happily enough and went on to marry the grinning son of auld Union Jack Harry, and sometimes lived happy ever after.

So that's my Nanny's story, and although she been dead for many a year, I have never forgotten her, But I have all those great memories of her. I can almost smell the house, with its mixtures of polish, and delicious smells of frying bread. When she died, I got her wedding ring, as it had an M inscribed inside it; I felt it was made for me. My small sister who's not really a midget, said it was bad luck to get married with her ring. But I went ahead and got married with the ring. She was right, as the marriage didn't work out. I ended up with a very similar life as Nanny, bringing up my child alone. Although I didn't ever wear a hairnet, or drawers, or an overall to save my clothes.

Saturdays

Saturdays had a certain smell when I was growing up in the fifties and sixties. A smell you didn't get on any other day of the week. It was a mixture of Jelly setting and marrowfat peas slowly softening in warm water with a white tablet, and she polish, and the smell of the sachet of shampoo which was in a cup with warm water to stretch it to shampoo all seven heads. All does smells mingling together gave this gorgeous aroma which was unique to Saturday.

Saturdays then was a very busy day of shopping and cleaning and bathing all in preparation for the big event which was Sunday. Sunday which had tree important events which were "THE MASS, THE ROAST, AND THE WALK." Saturdays then were as busy as Christmas now. When we kids awoke hearing the milkman, and realised it was a Saturday we somehow never felt like sleeping in as on school days. Of course, it was busy for the Mammy's with all that cleaning and shopping and feeding large families. This was pre supermarket days and most people didn't have cars except the doctor and the odd posh person. My Mother kept the old pram for this purpose, long after the youngest was walking. At the local shops on Saturdays, these mammy's attired in their colourful headscarves, heads bobbing up and down like busy ants. Warning the butcher if the meat wasn't tender, they would be bringing it back. Shaking their head-scarved heads at him and looking fierce. They would nod at each other as they went about their business, they usually brought one or other of the children to help them.

Our Saturday dinner was always the same, mince balls with potatoes. After the shopping was put away. The butter put in the big pot filled with cold water. That pot was a multipurpose pot it was also the pot which was used to bring the hot water up the stairs to fill the Saturday bath. It was also the Christmas pot used to boil the puddings. It stands now on my top shelf in retirement, as it has served us well over the years and deserves its place there. My Mother would stand with floured hands, in her piny, making the mince balls a tear running down her face from the cut onion, gently lowering them in the spitting dripping. Turning them as they browned and then at that moment adding the Bisto. If a toddler had become grisly, she would hoist it up on her left hip at the same time stirring a pot with her right hand. These Mammies then knew how to multitask before the word was invented.

After the dinner was cleared away My Father would ask "has anyone got homework to do. Four voices would answer," no "at the same time. Then the baths would begin. The girls first, the water was clean then, but by the time the fifth came it had gone a bit murky, But I don't think the boys minded too much. Each of us got a little of the watered-down shampoo, "Vosene". While this was all going on My Father would polish the shoes, while listening to the wireless. Polishing away, sometimes pausing, to laugh at the "Klitoroo kid." All those shoes highly polished and lined up in a row awaiting Sunday.

After the baths were finished, the Delph put away and the shoes shined, the Sunday clothes were laid out. White socks and clean white vests which only really stayed white for the day. Then the youngest were put to bed. And the two eldest allowed to stay up for the Saturday film. Thank God I was the eldest, I would sit in my flannelette nighty my feet under me cosily on the sofa *in anticipation of the film. Then the scullery door would be shut, for the day and the lights put out. The only light was the flickering fire casting shadows on the flowered wallpaper and the flicker of the little black and white TV, In the corner. The fire guard would be put in place to protect us from sparks. With the coal glowing and hissing breaking the silence, the film would begin. Bette Davies would look out at us, mesmerizing, with such classics as what ever happened to baby Jane. After the film my father would make toast for our supper. This was pre toaster days, so he used a toasting fork, made from the wire of the briquets. Warm butter would run down your fingers from the toast which we would lick off.*

All too soon Monday came along; Monday didn't seem to have any smell at all apart from porridge. Gloomy faces sat at the table worried about schoolwork not done. Mammy would look out the window for clouds worried about the weekly wash, and go and get the big pot, which she used for boiling the wash. We would all sit and sigh and wait for the next Saturday.

Nuclear War

I was born in 1953, so my childhood was spent in the fifties and sixty's, the pre computer days. The pre digital days, before mobiles, colour tele, and lap tops. We had to use our imagination, we had no option, really. Play involved skill, and much imagination. We engaged with one another, unlike the zombie like children of today, clicking madly on phones etc.

There were different seasons of play, January and February, you would see children with bikes or skates, or whatever they were lucky enough to get for Christmas. But then kids tended only to get one gift, not forgetting the orange. For some strange reason we all got an orange with our Christmas stocking.

Then the Spring, would see kids skipping and playing marbles. Of course, Summer would see us all going to the beach merrily in gangs together. Another favourite was catching bees in summer time. It took great skill, with an empty jam jar you crept quietly to the unsuspecting bee, gorging on a flower. And hey presto you quickly captured it with the lid. The problem was, when you had a full jar of angry bees trying to get one more in, without letting the lot out. Great skill not to mention fool hearty.

But my favourite game of all was what I called nuclear war. Sometime in the sixty's there was imminent danger of a cold war with Russia. All homes were issued with a small book, called *"An Bas"*. A sort of guide, in the event of a nuclear war. I wasn't sure what nuclear was, but it sounded great excitement to me. Especially if it meant no school.

In those days I went every Sunday to my grannies with my younger sister. My Nannie as we called her, had hung the little book on a nail in the hall. Every Sunday, we took it down, and studied it. It showed pictures of fall out coloured pink on roofs, and houses. It stated after war the fall out is dangerous and people are to stay indoors. I decided this would be a Sunday, and we would be at my Nannies and of course, no school due to the fall out. The book also advised, what to have ready in order to survive the fall out. I studied it with military precision. Tinned food was needed, as no one could go to shops. My Nannie indulged me by buying in loads of tinned food. I decided which room we would live in the one least likely to have fall out on top. We would have a radio and lots of books of course. Sometimes I couldn't wait. There was a small problem though. My grannie's toilet was outside and of course we couldn't go out because of the fall out. I pondered this problem greatly. It kept me awake at night. No general could have given it more thought. Living with a toilet bucket was out of the question of course. But so was going outside in the fall out. I wondered a small hole in the wall perhaps. Daylight often broke, and I still hadn't solved the toilet problem.

Nuclear war never came to pass of course, and I never solved the problem. Instead, I started to have a great interest in pop music and of course boys. I pursued this interest as avidly as I had the nuclear war. One thing always puzzled me though whatever did my Grannie do with all those tins of food we had ready for the nuclear war.?

The Secret

"*Well, you kept that quiet, didn't you?*" *65 years, it's a long time*, to keep a secret. Oh, you must have been burdened with it. We will never know now. She left it for a month after you went, to tell us. *that caused uproar, I can tell you!*". You told her you were taking it to the grave with you, and you did.

We went to see her after she rang, I must admit I didn't like her very much, I'm afraid I didn't feel any bond with her at all. May felt very hurt, that you had not told her. As for Phil well you know her, the drama queen, angry and phoning around to see was it true. You would have hated that, but you know that one never could keep her mouth shut. As for me I just felt very sad for you.

It's true what they say truth is stranger than fiction. But the strange thing for me is, why call me the same name? We joked about it, Margaret one and Margaret two, I suddenly lost my status as the eldest. It must have been terrible for you back in the forties to give up your child. It explains a lot though. Why you were so protective of us, and how strict you were with us when it came to boys.

Is heaven all that it's cracked up to be? Or is it there at all? Like Thomas, I doubt it very much, unlike you, with your faith. You held on to it like a drowning man, clinging to a raft, no matter what life threw at you. No matter how I argued with you, by the way sorry for that. You will be pleased to know I often don't listen to the news now either, although I used to tell you that you had to be informed, how bossy I was at times.

I packed all your clothes up and brought them back the same charity shops where you bought them. But I couldn't part with your coat. That coat which saw so many masses it could probably say mass itself. Hope you're being rewarded for all that praying. I left the coat just hanging there, maybe it's still there, who knows. I don't go to the graveyard as you must know, but, on your anniversary, if I'm near a church I light a candle for you, instead as you were always a candle person.

Not a lot happening down here same old, wars, famine, crooked politicians. No wonder you never listened to the news. But there are good things too, like a nice chat with friends, a good book, a film, watching the garden grow. I have to end here that's all the news for now, maybe will see each other one day, but not too soon I hope as I have a lot of living to do, from your ever-loving daughter, Margaret two.

A Cowboy and a Dog called Trigger

He had decided to come back, to *Eireinn Go brath*. He had spent over 30 years in London, working hard on building sites. A hard life, working in all weathers, waiting for the start, rain dripping down his neck. Life in Camden town was hard then, and the men even harder, they worked hard and played harder still. He had seen what had happened when the body gave out, and how the men often ended up in bedsits, drinking their last days away and dreaming of Eireann go Braith. He'd had a scare when he'd got a clot in his leg. After his mother died and the flat was empty, he took his chance, and the ferry home. The only things he had to show for his years of toil, were his much-loved DVDs of cowboy films, and the clothes he stood up in, his wife had the benefit of his worldly goods.

He; d always loved western films, his heroes were *"Clint Eastwood"*. When he was younger h; ed practised walking in a cowboy gait so much that it stuck, and he now walked permanently like that, which gave him the nick name cowboy on the sites in London. Den didn't mind that, he was a tall and rangy man with an easy smile, and laughing brown eyes. He soon got to know everyone in the area. He went on benefit, he felt he'd deserved it; Ireland owed him after all, as with a lot of young men in the seventies he'd had to emigrate, so it was his due he felt.

He ripped up the carpet in his mother's house, to make it more range like. He had the gas cut off, as why spend money on fuel when there were fields full of logs ready for the taking. He found himself a dog which he called Trigger; he was devoted to him as Trigger was to him. Early morning would find them both in the fields collecting logs. But it wasn't just a field to Den it was the prairie, and Trigger was a prairie dog. *" Gide up der Trigger"*, he'd say, his saw over his shoulder, ready for another day on the prairie. He became a familiar figure in the prairie field. People said hello to him He'd reply, *" howdy"*. He trained trigger to pull the logs, just like a prairie dog. He stacked the logs up against the fireplace, till they reached the ceiling. The flat now really looked like a ranch, he felt. He rummaged in skips and found some great treasures. One was an old kettle, which he would lay on top of the fire, for tea in the evenings, while he watched, *"A Fist full of Dollars"*, Trigger happily curled up at his feet.

Sometimes the social security would want to see him about finding a job. But Den was wise to their ploy. He would show up with a two-day growth on his chin, an old hankie round his neck, which he would use to wipe sweat off his brow. The young girl would look at him and wonder where to place him. He had no computer experience, he didn't own a suit or even a shirt, and she looked at him in his old jeans and cowboy jacket, in despair, and felt shed smelled smoke from him. Well shed say, *"you will be hearing from us"* as she put his file in the section," *hard to place"*. Den would go out laughing to himself, and go home to the ranch and shave.

It was a cold Jan day when Den saw the girl sitting on a bench and crying. It was so cold that Den had his trapper hat on, and the girl was shivering holding a can of beer for dear life. She was a pretty girl, with dark hair and blue vulnerable eyes. She told Den about rowing with her mother, and having no place to live, as they shared a beer together. Den was partial to a beer as well. She had organised somewhere to live but that wasn't till tomorrow. Her name was Ailsa; she told him as they walked back to the ranch. He gave her sausages and beans, as all good cowboys know what's good for a body. She sat at the fire with Den and felt safe in the firelight, with Trigger beside them.

Next day she moved in temporary with a friend Shane. He was very different to Den, a smooth talker. He didn't like Den he didn't approve of him and his life style. He tried his upmost to stop the friendship with Den and Ailsa, calling him *"a cowboy"*. He felt he could sort out Ailsa's life, much better. And gave her his advice daily, He rang her up all the time and tried to prise her away from Den. Den realised he was a controller, but he let Ailsa make up her own mind as he didn't believe in forcing people, Den was a free spirit, and believed in freedom.

One evening he was expecting Ailsa to come over, but she didn't arrive, Den decided to ring her but to his surprise, Shane answered her phone. He could hear Ailsa in the background, trying to get to her phone. Den said to Shane, *" let her go or I'm coming round to get her"*, but the phone went dead. *" C'mon boy, "* Den said to Trigger, we have to rescue a lady in distress, Trigger wagged his tail following. Dan walked along singing, *"do not forsake me oh my darling"*, as in his mind it was High noon and it wasn't Ailsa but *Grace Kelly*, and it was about honour.

He got to the chic apartment of Shane and once more rang Ailsa mobile but again Shane answered, he could hear her shouts in the background. *If you don't let her, go, I'm ringing the police*, he told Shane. Standing there he wished it could be a shoot-out between them as in the Wild West, but instead rang the police signing. After a while the police arrived at the scene, and to Dens surprise a policeman said to him, *"Your the guy who gathers logs"*, Dan was pleased he was so well known, he grinned to himself. Shane released Ailsa when the police entered, *"shouting I'll get you"* to Den. Den laughed as he took Ailsa by the arm, leading her through the prairie to the ranch, a dog called Trigger following behind.

Dave The Prince of Tides

The world is full of little people; I'm one of them. Little people with dreams, however small or insignificant. Actually, that makes up 95% of the human race, I read somewhere only 5 precent will be remembered. Like Hitler and Putin, and who wants that? Most of us want little things, have dreams, and will only be remembered by the people who lives we touched, who loved us, had an impact on our lives. So, I want to write about someone who was very important to me. I always thought I would see him again, just to chat with him really, as he was my first real love and I have such great memories of him and our life together.

I knocked on a door one morning in Jersey sometime in 1975. I'll explain, I was 22 and had gone to Jersey with my sister to work as silver service waitresses, even though we were not. My father got some headed paper from our local hotel. And wrote great glowing references for us and due to his lies we got the jobs! However, we were sacked within a month! The owner of the hotel was puzzled and said with gritted teeth "*The Hayward Sisters*", I can't *understand it, they had such great references*"! My sister went back home to Ireland, after all she was only seventeen, but me being a very mature twenty-two-year-old, decided to stick it out and stay. That day, I was looking for work as I was walking about, I passed a house where I had been at a party the night before, and decided to knock on the door. To my surprise, this bearded man opened the door, he had not been at the party, but invited me in. Me," being an adventurous kind of person, *who doesn't see the mud and just jumps in the puddle"* said yes. We clicked immediately; I loved his Yorkshire accent. He told me," *He had never met a young Irish person, only old women in shawls, who smoked pipes."* Knocking on that door would be the start of something that would last seven years. Sometimes destiny is as simple as an impulse of knocking on a door. We spent the day together, and many days and nights together, and decided to live together, as the house wasn't suitable with just single men. Through a friend of Dave's, there was a tiny flat in the centre. But it required paying two months' rent in advance. I had found a job at the time, (picking flowers on a farm) and Dave was a carpenter, but we had to come up with the money very quickly. There was a cabin at the building site where he worked, where the guys had tea. We sneaked in at night, and slept there, we even had a tiny cooker to have tea and soup, but we had to get up early before the men arrived. Dave walked me down the road and then walked back to the same place, acting as if he just arrived for work!

Our cabin days were short, and we moved into our tiny flat. Dave asked the landlord for permission to do some alterations, but was in shock when he arrived to see a gaping hole where the door had been. Dave was putting the kitchen in the tiny hall, and needed the door at the other side. I went to an auction to look for a small sofa, and found two, as I couldn't decide which to buy, so I bought both! Thus began my love affair with auctions and second-hand shops! There were also the contents of a paint shop for sale, which I bid for and got for 20 pounds. Dave picked up the paint in his van, and was aghast at the colours. Puke yellow, poo green, blinding pink, about fifty to a hundred tins, we stored them down in a cellar. They would later save us when we fell on hard times. Dave suggested to the landlord he paint the house outside instead of paying the rent! I think he mixed the puke yellow and poo green together to get a nice pee colour. I often wonder years later, if it still the same colour. We had access to the garden out the back. It contained the contents of an old stone shed, which had fallen down on top of the soil. But I painstakingly, bucket by bucket cleared it until soil appeared. We then grew tomatoes, salad, chives and onions. Jerseys' climate is ideal for growth, as it enjoys about 9 months of sunshine in the year.

So, began our Idyllic life together in this beautiful island in the sun. We spent many happy hours on the beach. Dave just loved the sea, boats, fishing and swimming. We would go fishing for razer fish, which is quite a skill, as you must find a hole in the sand and pour salt into it and wait the razer fish pops his head up, being careful not to cast a shadow that the fish will see you. When it does you have to grab the head and pull it out. You have to boil the razer fish for hours, and even then, they are very tough, I never found it worth the trouble. He loved picking periwinkles off the rocks, you boil them and when they are ready you have to use a pin to get the little snail-like creature out. I can still see him with his pin gorging on them.

Sometime later Dave went into business for himself, and had a few men working for him, and we were doing quite well. He bought a little green sport car, a Sunbeam Alpine which he said was for me but as I didn't drive, it really was for him. Though I enjoyed racing round the island with the top down, with him driving. After that we got a dog called Jason, then a ferret called Jet, and a budgie called Pecker. The ferret he got in Ireland, and made a box for it and flew it on the plane as baggage. We arrived back in Jersey but Jet didn't, he was on the next plane, hence the name. He wanted to hunt rabbits so Jason and Jet were brought to the dunes on the 5-mile road. I never went as I couldn't watch; I stayed home with Pecker. When I got home from work, I would find skinned rabbits in the sink, but I still remember the delicious rabbit pie and stews they made. Dave was a kind of Grizzly Adams, crossed with Neptune, with his wild curly hair and beard. One thing I remember is his sense of humour. We both laughed at each other and together. I found his Yorkshire accent and idioms funny as he did my Irish ones. He called me *"our lass"* other funny things were *"will I Eck (heck} as like"* and *"have you seen me at(hat}"*.

His dream was to have a boat, and fish for lobsters to sell to the French market. I was fully behind his decision to sell his business and buy a boat. Little did I know at that time, just how it would affect our lives and in actual fact would be the end of us and our life in Jersey. For a start the boat was a second hand one, which needed a lot of work, but as a carpenter and also with a knowledge of engines, he set out daily to refurbish it. I was working packing tomatoes in a warehouse, at the time which was well paid, so we managed to survive on one wage, that is in the beginning! Nobody realises the work involved to starting a lobster fisherman business. The lobster pots have to be covered with rubber to prevent salt corrosion; guess who did most of the weaving the rubber from tyres, around the frames, little ole me of course! You also have to have about ten strings of pots, each one with eight pots on each string, to really make a living. At this time a guy he knew went into business with him. They both loved the sea, were well suited and they worked very hard to get it all together. The boat was finally sea worthy, shining with a coat of varnish and in the harbour. But not everyone was as happy as they were, the other fishermen resented the two Englishmen coming into their territory. Fishing is a closed shop, with families of fishermen going back generations.

So started their lives as fishermen. It's a hard life both physically and mentally. Dave was gone for hours each day, as you have to catch the tides. He lost so much weight winching up the pots. Things went wrong, as the French started to buy lobster from Canada so the market value went down. On the bright side we ate a lot of lobster, (lobster salad, lobster stew, lobster fishcake) so much so that after a while I told him to" *bring home the bait*", which is mackerel! With the fish he brought home and the tomatoes I got; we ate very well. When things got really bad, my auction paint came to the rescue! One night there was a big storm, the boat came apart from its moorings (or was cut by rival fishermen) and was a wreck. We were devastated. Dave's dream was shattered. All that work gone in the blink of an eye. We decided to leave Jersey, and bring Jason to his Mam, while we would go to Europe to work for a while, and get enough money for another boat. Carpenters were being paid great sums of money, in Germany and Holland. So that was the plan to make some money and go back.

We got the boat to England, and drove up to Yorkshire. On the way Dave rang a friend back in Jersey at a garage, (no mobile phones then) The friend told him we had won the turkey in our local bar! Luck! As we drove, Dave said to me *"at least we still have the car"* After a while smoke started to bellow out of the engine. Yes, the engine had gone, we had to leave Jason at the garage and get a guest house for the night. Next day we picked up the dog and travelled by train to Redcar. Dave said he would get another engine for the Sunbeam when we got back on our feet, I would love to give you a happy ending, but I can't, it didn't end happy. We never did get back to Jersey, or get the car back. We lived together in Holland for a while, but it wasn't the same any more. We had lost our home, and Dave had lost his dream. We stayed together for another two years breaking up and then making up again. Finally, Dave went back to England, Holland never really suited him, he was too wild and free. I stayed there for 27 years, and lost touch with him.

For years I tried through social media to track him down, as I often thought about him. Finally, just yesterday I found his brother. Reader, you are not going to like this, but he told me Dave had died in 2010. But the good part is he got another boat; one he lived on. He also got a new partner and had a son (that part I'm a bit jealous of, *"couldn't he have waited another 30 years for me? Men!"*) I'm happy he found happiness in the end. I'm feeling very sad, I never expected to feel so sad. But I'm so glad I knocked on that door that day in 1975, it brought me a lot of joy and happiness, also a lot of sorrow, but that's life.

The Honeymoon

Most people's honeymoons are memorable mainly for romantic reasons. But their honeymoon was memorable for quite different reasons. In retrospect she believes it was when she first saw the enormous differences between them.

The plane landed on the sun basked beautiful Island of Corfu where they were to spend 2 weeks honeymoon. The taxi took them to their accommodation which was right by the see. It was rustic little house where chickens ran round the small yard. All very charming and very Greek, there was a restaurant a few minutes' walk away where tables were laid out on the sand some even reaching the waves. They served beautiful Greek dishes there. The first few days they just relaxed sitting at a little table the waves softly lapping around them. It was very romantic so let them have that time reader, as what will happen to them soon, will be entirely different.

He was a keen sailor so it was decided they would hire a boat. So, they set off one morning with their passports to hire a boat. She wore a sundress and brought sun cream and a book ready for a lovely day on the beautiful blue sea. They sailed happily round the Island for a while looking at the lovely little bays on the way. After some time, they decided to stop a while at one of the tiny bays. She spotted one and he steered the boat towards it and cut the engine.

Suddenly a shot rang out. They both stared, startled, around them. There were three soldiers on the beach in battle position with guns pointing at them. It was a night mare. She suddenly jumped to the bottom of the boat praying, becoming a born again catholic, OH Mary all the saints, help us. He on the other hand stood up, and said, *"we are tourists, English"*. To this day she can never decide if he was brave or merely arrogant. She thought then as she lay flat down what kind of fool have, I married they will kill him. She wondered if there been a military coup in Greece.

The soldiers indicated to them to come ashore. She climbed down the small ladder and he followed her. When they reached the beach, they could see the red stars on their kaki hats. What does this mean she wondered? They were made to sit while the soldiers held their guns pointed at them. They heard the word Albania. *"OH God"*, she thought was not in Greece how on earth did we get here. She tried to remember what she knew of Albania there was a safety card on the boat saying beware of Albanian hospitality. The only other thing she could think of was *"Mother Theresa"* but these soldiers with their shaven heads bore little resemblance to her. Trying to converse with them was useless as they didn't speak any English. They indicated to her husband they wanted passports so he went back on the boat to get them. He whispered to her; he had hidden their money in his sock. She looked amazed at him, wondering how he could think of money at a time like this.

One of the soldiers went away in a land rover. The others stayed they mentioned interpreter. It had become very hot even the soldiers looked hot and lowered their guns a bit. One of them handed her water from a bottle there were bits of green moss in it but she drank it and thanked him She offered her husband the water, but he said I'm not drinking that. She hissed at him, *"don't be so arrogant were their captives"*. She wondered would they ever get out she thought of stories in the paper where people went missing and were never seen again.

Hours went by and the soldiers seemed more relaxed if it wasn't for the uniform and guns, it would have been just another lovely sunny day at the beach. She began to think, maybe after all they won't kill us as they smiled at her and offered her water now and then. She began to feel more relaxed, even a little bored in fact, and picked up her book. Her husband suddenly noticed her reading and exclaimed, *"you're not reading are you in amazement."* Those differences again reader.

Sometime later, her husband tried to communicate with them, with a stick in the sand. He indicated his watch, and made a circle in the sand, meaning a day the soldier caught on and made 3 circles in the sand. Her husband despairing said, *"three days"!* She said to him,*" oh never mind if they keep us for 3 days maybe we will see the town, and we will be able to see how communism works"* as she was always interested in communism. He again looked at her in amazement and said, *"you want to spend three days of our honeymoon in a communist jail"!* "Well,", she replied meekly.

Dusk had fallen when the sound of the land rover returned and a pleasant looking man got out of it. He was wearing normal civilian clothes and his head wasn't shaven. He said, *"welcome to Albania"*, in perfect English. He was the interpreter. Her husband sighed in relief. He studied their passports and looking at her husband's British one said, *"Oh England, Margaret Thatcher"*. *"We don't like England"*, and he then looked at her Irish passport and said, *"Bobby sands, people fighting for freedom we like Ireland"*. She tried not to smirk. He explained how close Albania was to Corfu a couple of miles only. So much for her husband's navigation.

They were both amazed when he produced a propaganda book. He showed a photo in it with people digging in the fields and said, *"before the revolution"* and then a photo with a tractor and said, *"after the revolution"*.

Soon after they were allowed to go. By this time, it was dark as darkness falls early there. They pointed to the lights in the distance and told them, it was Corfu. They wished them well. They headed for the lights and arrived on a beach to the amazement of the diners and waiter at the restaurant there. It wasn't the place where they left at all but further north, they realised how Far they had drifted. Her husband parked the boat on the sand They both looked bedraggled with hair askew, looking like Robinson Crusoe, A waiter ran to them and asked, *"where u come from"*-= **Albania**, they replied.

A Woman, Most Royal

I think of her fondly, my mother-in-law, now long gone. Mostly I laugh, or smile when I think of her. She was such a character, full of eccentric ways and contradictions. She worked for many years as a cook, for royals such as the Spencer family. In fact, she had become more royal than the royals themselves! Her accent was that of the Queen, she greeted you with, "my dear", but occasionally her Yorkshire broad accent would show through, and a "bloody ell" would slip out. Of course, her favorite color was royal blue, and her China was Royal Daulton.

When I first went to stay at Sandbeck Park, with my young son, I was amazed, I felt I had arrived on the set for Emmerdale Farm, the soap opera! Sandbeck Park is the home of the Lord and Lady Scarborough, an impressive estate of many acres. Each staff member has a home there, known as a tithe cottage, where the house was theirs, until death. There was the cooks house, the pheasant's keepers house, the valets house, to name but a few. The houses were charming, but old and damp. My mother-in-law knitted herself a hat, which she wore when cleaning the bathroom, as it was so cold there, this amused me so much! The whole estate had been landscaped by Capability Brown and his hallmark Maple tree, stood in front of the main house. It even had its own graveyard, for discerning royal corpses. All this amazed me as an Irish person, used only to a President. My mother-in law informed me that as a result of the *Labour* government, heavy taxation on estates such as this, had reduced these people to organize pheasant hunt weekends for the finance, in order to manage such large estates. *"My dear, it is terrible vexing that they must be treated so",* followed by *"bloody Labour"* She was such a loyal royal woman! Although when I stayed there in the eighties, Thatcher (the milk slasher) was in power, and there were major battles with the miners going on. My mother-in-law greatly approved *of Mrs. Thatcher,* in fact they looked and spoke alike, always carried a handbag, they even had the same blue rinsed hair. One thinks of true -blue conservative. She had the same distain for the miners, and would never give money to their cause. When she saw a collection box she walked past, muttering under her breathe, *"bloody miners".*

The English habit of "Tea Drinking" was staunchly adhered to in my mothers-in-law house, the tea tray was always on the ready. Complete with linen cloth, on which rested the Royal Daulton China cups and saucers. Never mugs, *"so vulgar my dear".* It was an hourly ritual; the clink of China was heard on the hour. China's economy was greatly boosted by my mother-in-law, In the evenings she and Sid, (her second husband, the first is a long story I'll tell you later) played cards or did the crossword while listening to the *Ink Spots.* The memory of hearing the song *"why do you whisper green grass"* still makes me smile. They consulted each other with clues for the crossword, type of bird, *"S, U, Somat, somat, somat, E S?* It *t*ook me awhile to realize, that *"soma"t* meant something, in the Yorkshire dialect. Vitamins were never lacking in her house, with her gardener husband bringing fresh vegetables daily. She loved to tell you when having dinner, "they were growing half an hour ago", with a proud air. She also was an avid reader, of *Catherine Cookson,* and asked me was it true what she read in one, "my dear, did Irish people put the pot of potatoes on the table". She shyly told me that she liked *Harold Robbins* as well, a noted raunchy writer. She confessed to me that when she finished one of his books, rather than letting neighbors know about this hidden habit of depravity. "What I do, my dear, *I tear up the pages and wrap them in used tea bags before putting them in the bin to hide the evidence from neighbors and bin men*".

My mother-in laws' life was not an easy one, in fact the opposite. She was nineteen when she first married during the war. Her husband she told me*," Who had delusions of grandeur, would never eat his fish and chips out of newspaper, had to have a plate,"*, went off to war. He never came back, he wasn't killed in action, he just went to Canada. There he married a Canadian woman, not bothering to get divorced from his English wife, and completely forgetting he had a son. Thus, my poor mother-in-law was left high and dry. At that time there was no social security so she had to find work to accommodate her son, my husband. Being a resourceful woman, that she did. She found work as a cook in a prestigious boarding school, which was a live-in position, solving her housing and food problem, as well as her son's education in one quick swoop. So, my husband acquired a BBC accent as well, which in the beginning I found sexy, but in the end the *"my dear"* began to grate on my nerves. So much so, I had to send him and his accent packing, leaving me in the same position as my mother-in-law. That's another story, this one is solely my mother's-in-law.

Eventually she left that post, upped herself by being a cook for the Spencer household, where she met Sidney, her future husband, who was the gardener there. They married and had many happy years of the best of vegetables cooked by her expert hands. What romance! Sid was quite willing to be bossed around by his wife, as by then she had acquired the assertive manner and accent.

One Summers day, my husband planned a trip to Althorp, the Spencer house, (well more of a mansion really) This delighted her and Sid, as they had met there, when she was the cook and he the gardener. She told us, *"Sid and I used to go on trips there on the train, but my dear these days the seats on trains are so hairy its uncomfortable don't you find my dear?* I didn't answer as I needed time to wonder what *"hairy seats"* were exactly. Althorp had become a popular place to visit since *Diane Spencer* had become, *Princess of Wales*. Of course, that pleased the *Spencer* family who took full advantage of the commercial implications of that. Here and there, there were carefully placed framed photos of a smiling Diane, in the very tastefully decorated rooms, complete with Persian carpets, (which it was forbidden to walk on), I felt they were deliberately placed in prominent positions, to catch the public eye. As we waked up the staircase where portraits of its ancestry hung in gold gilded frames. My Mother-in- delighted in telling me the family history. We reached the top, and to my surprise there was portrait which was totally out of place, without the antique look of the other pictures. This was the present Lady Spencer sporting a mini skirt, I was informed by my mother-in law with distain. *"Oh, my dear how vulgar"*, she said, with disapproval, she is the daughter of the writer *Barbara Cartland*. She then tells me *Barbara Cartland* had groomed all her daughters to make such matches. I thought to myself," *how odd English people were with such customs"*. Having seen the house, we went for a well- deserved cup of tea, of course. A coffee house was recently constructed to cater to the many visitors who were flocking there since Diane's rise to fame. On the shelves were bottles of wine for sale, with a label saying Althorp! As we were sitting drinking the inevitable tea, who should come in but the lady from the portrait, the present Lady

Spencer. To my husband and I great horror, my mother-in-law beckoned to her as she passed. In her best Margaret Thatcher voice, she said, *"my husband and I have given thirty-four years of service to Althorp"* My husband blinked, I blinked and Lady Spencer blinked, then she smiled, a strange little smile maybe slightly condescending. I realized quite a lot of people were staring at us. It got worse, My Mother-in-law then said in the same tone of voice, *"One finds it almost impossible to find good servants these days".* My husband gulped, I gulped, Lady Spencer smiled as she walked away, with a click of her stiletto heel. We decided to leave at this point; in case she would speak again. My husband kept his head down as he paid for the tea; I busied myself under the table, and then we hastily left, both of us shaking slightly. My Mother-in-law remarked in the car, *"my dear, that was a lovely day, wasn't it, did you both enjoy it?".*

One particular event always springs to mind when I think of her. It makes me laugh, but it also gives me the shivers. To this day I don't know how I endured it! I offered to take her and Sid to Paris along with my two-year-old (diagnosed as hyper-active) son for a weekend. My own mother was aghast, *"that difficult woman and your wild child, oh no!"* I lived in Holland, and they were there on holiday, so this involved a five-hour journey by bus. That was exhausting in itself, my son constantly bopping me on the head, with his empty bottle, an endearing little habit of his. When we reached Paris, I was duly sent to reception with a flask for the *"inevitable,"* tea. I realized we were in the Pigalle area, as I looked out and saw the ladies of the nights touting for business. I said *"quick Sid look,"* there's one getting in a car. For my mother-in-law, a secret lover of *Harold Robbins* novels, this was a step too far in reality. She held her hands to her face saying, *"my dear, whatever will they say at Sandbeck"* I didn't really see any of the sights of Paris, as at every stop of the coach tour, it was "tea, my *dear"* and by the time I fetched it, it was time to get back on the coach. At one particular stop as I waited in the queue," she loudly shouted to me *"Earl Grey my dear"* at a fast-food café in Paris! But standards are standards, and she was quite surprised they didn't have the brand. I went home exhausted, having not seen much of Paris, but, however, I drank a lot of tea, so not all was lost.

Many years have passed since she died but my memories of her and of Sid are good, happy ones. Another of her attributions was her kindness, she had a big heart as big as her passion for Royality.

Mrs Glaudeman

The doorbell rang. Mrs Gloudeman stood at the door about to open it. She knew it would be the new home help. She thought, "*I hope it's not like the last one they sent, she had a nose piercing for God's sake". She didn't look too clean either.* Mrs Gloudeman had a war going with dirt, she hated it. She soon sent her, and her nose piercing packing. She told them, to send someone else next time, someone normal who could work.

The girl stood at the other side of the door with trepidation. "*As a home help, you never knew who you would get.*"

Mrs Gloudeman opened the door and thought well, "*this one is not too bad and ushered her in.*" Mrs Gloudeman had short steel grey hair, and small brown eyes like buttons, that seemed to glitter when she was angry. She showed the girl around the small apartment, and showed her where the dusters were, but she would help her with the dusting and light work. Mrs Gloudeman didn't like idleness either. That way she could keep her eye on the girl, and make sure she was doing it right.

The girl looked round at the spotless apartment and thought, "*how clean it was*" and to her mind didn't need cleaning at all. She wished, "*her own house would ever look like that that*". She picked up the duster and together with Mrs Gloudeman began to clean the imaginary dust. They cleaned imaginary smudges off doors as well.

At coffee time, Mrs Gloudeman told the girl about the operation she had had. The worst part was not to be able to go out, as she was still quite weak.

The girl thought,*" she's not so bad after all and how awful it would be not to go out and do the everyday things like shopping."*

The next week when the girl came again, she offered to take the old lady out in the wheel chair, to the supermarket. Although, she wasn't sure if she could manage it, and if it was allowed by the office. But the girl often broke the rules.

Mrs Gloudeman was so happy to be out and about. She was quite pleased with the girl after all, even if she wasn't the very best of cleaners. The girl sometimes didn't see dust but she was polite and willing.

Mrs Gloudeman and the girl grew quite close over the months. At coffee times, Mrs Gloudeman would tell the girl about her life. The story she told her one day the girl has never forgotten.

Mrs Gloudeman got married at the start of the war. Soon after the country was under the jack boot. Swastikas were flying all round, and times were very hard. Like a lot of men Mrs Gloudeman's husband was sent to Germany. Food was scarce and Mrs Gloudeman found she was pregnant. But Mrs Gloudeman was made of stern stuff. She cleaned and dusted imagery dust and made the best of things. Mrs Gloudeman had relatives out of town with a small allotment. She made her way out there sometimes, to get a few carrots or some small thing. Soon after her baby girl was born. Mrs Gloudeman had a photo of her husband in a frame a very well dusted frame. She pointed to it all the time telling the little girl, "*pa pa*". She hadn't heard from him for a long time as towards the end of the war post had stopped. She put her little girl in a pram and walked to the farm to get some veg. Soldiers were about to stop her on her way back. Mrs Gloudeman's little brown eyes glittered at them; they told her to go on: She had hidden some potatoes under the baby's blanket. It was very well known, the Germans would take the food from you, yes, that was a very hard time for everyone; People were forced to take up floorboards, for fuel to burn for warmth

Finally, the war ended. The allies dropped bread down from planes. Mrs Gloudeman said she had never tasted better it felt like it was sent from heaven.

Months passed and no word of Mrs Gloudeman's husband had not returned; she had to presume him dead. One day, as she was returning with the little girl to her street the little girl kept saying "*Pa Pa*" and there on the door step was Mrs Gloudemans husband. The little girl had recognised him from the photo.

The girl finished her coffee, and felt a tear in her eye.

Soon after she was moved to another client. She promised she would call and see her but life got in the way.

Many years have passed the girl is now a middle-aged woman but she has never forgotten Mrs Gloudeman. She still doesn't see dust but sometimes wipes an imagery smudge from a door.

She feels sure Mrs Gloudeman is in heaven. In the dust free part; where the angels are never idle, and don't have nose piercings, and where you get to eat the bread the allies dropped every day.

Adventure in India

As the airplane taxied down the runway to a stop, I noticed a few drops of rain on the window. Rain! In India! In July. My son said," *Mom it's raining*", with an amazed air, I replied its warm rain, he nodded in the accepting way a six year tend to do, my friend Bernie looking guilty told me he had been there for the nine months when it's not monsoon! Oh well bring it on, it's another experience.

When we got outside the airport building, what hits you is the smell, it's like no other, a mixture of smoky fires jasmine, curries, and animal dung all mixed up to give the exotic flavour which is India. I wasn't prepared for the traffic in Bombay. Drivers play dodging death at every corner, with their brightly coloured cars, decorated with Christmas lights, blasting music loudly and beeping horns, it's like a giant carnival. Our bus drove through plastic bag city for over an hour. I looked out the windows in amazement at the ragged city teeming with life, people actually lived there in the bags we throw our rubbish out in! We finally reached the centre of Bombay, buildings had green moss on them which didn't show them at their best, at monsoon time. I stared in fright as about twenty youths tried to bring us to a hotel, pulling at us and jabbering "I Have best Hotel Madam" They were hotel touts, we chose one at random and walked with him there through the bustling streets. Beggars held their hands out saying Allah Allah, some without limbs, a lot of them had a white film over their eyes, nearly blind, with cataracts, which is a simple operation, but I don't suppose they have a national health plan here. I started to feel overwhelmed by all of it. *"My God a month of seeing this, how could I bear it"*, and this is only day one! The young hotel tout Ragi, who was a lovely young man walked alongside me I noticed a clicking sound coming from him and looked down at his feet. He wore flip flops, well kind of, the whole heel was missing, and his heels touched the ground as he walked! I suppose you could say he had flip without flop! He asked me where I was from, I told him I was Irish not expecting him to have heard of our small country so far away. He shocked me by saying *"Yes I have read Trinity madam"* What a contradiction India is, a humble hotel tout without flop in his flip flops, had read Trinity, not only that, when I asked him did, he find it bigoted, he replied "on the contrary Madam".

We reached our supposed "good hotel" which had much to be desired, grey sheets, not to mention tiles missing off the shower wall! It looked to me like the prison in the film Midnight Express! Well, I had had enough for the moment I was going to open my duty-free gin and have a stiff one, with all the shocks Id had. What I didn't know there would be plenty more to come. I then heard a hissing sound coming from the door, I opened it to find a family camped in the hall way cooking chapattis their blankets laid out on the flour. Bernie my friend informs me that you can rent space on the hotel flour.

Next day we began to explore Bombay, which in parts resemble London as they have inherited the red buses since the colonial days. "Well, a very poor London" Giant boards proclaiming things like "The people will frown the sugar is brown" lay along the motorway, I never did find out what they meant. Toilet paper is nowhere to be seen, so you wash yourself muslin fashion. My son quickly adopted to this, he fact he loved it! To begin with we loved the curries and tandoori, but I had a feeling we would tire of them, as there wasn't much evidence of European fare around. I was beginning to get used to the beggars, it's amazing how quick you acclimatise. Another strange thing about India is although it was colonised by England, the people seem to embrace Englishness. I saw, many schools with names like Saint Anne's, and school uniforms, it's as if it's an imitation of England. They don't seem to have the bitterness which we Irish has. I looked forward to going to Goa where I felt it would be easier, with its beaches.

Goa is beautiful with its beaches and coconut trees surrounding them. But you have to be very careful as the coconut pickers, who are slung in a sort of jacket attached to the trees very high up, just throw them down on the ground. You could end up with a bad case of concussion. Bernie had stayed here before and we were going to stay at the place where he had been. The man greeted us nodding his head from side to side, which I still don't know if it's a yes or no. He showed us a beautiful pink tiled bathroom, I began to smile but then stopped as he said " *next year I get water*", still nodding his head. So, it was to be an outside toilet of sorts. It had no ceiling, but four walls and a bucket affair, the back wall had an opening at the bottom, for your waste to fall out where the household pig soon cleared it up! We named that pig" *Herbie*" the sanitation man. My son Philip loved greeting him," *hi Herbie*" he'd say when we saw him. India is not for the fainthearted! One of the most memorable times was in the evenings at the town square, which was a big tree! guys would gather and bring you places for a few rupees on the back of a motor bike. We had heard of a restaurant out of town, which showed Faulty Towers episodes and served plain food like roast beef. I will always remember sitting on the back of the motor bike, with the night black as ink, and fire flies could be seen whirling by. Another great evening, we were walking and heard beautiful eastern music coming from a sort of chapel. It was a sort of Hindu festival, they invited us in, and gave us some rice cake to eat, how hospitable of them, as we had the stray dog with us that my son had adopted!

We went to Pangi market to get supplies. There, a part aside from the food section, that's for tailors and they repair everything, including flip flops! I saw a huge pile of soles and a pile of toe pieces. India knows all about job creation, nothing is wasted or thrown out everything is repaired giving jobs to all. It's not our consumer society. I was quite taken back to see the butcher sitting among his meat and using his foot to slice it. Yuk! Now I know why they warn you about getting food poisoning.

Finally, we went to Delhi, it took three days from Goa by train to get there, but what an incredible journey. It was never boring; we went through states called Utter Pradesh and other strange sounding names. We had bunk beds, my son took the top and when he was bored, he just slept, every so often he would pop his head down and say "are we there yet?" But one morning he was looking glum and when I asked him the matter, "he said I'm worried about my dog" the street dog he had adopted in Goa. I reassured him that the dog would soon find another tourist. Every so often the train would stop for an hour or so, I never tired of the sights I saw. Young boys sold cold drinks from aluminium buckets, including gin! There was a strange gurney on a platform covered in a white sheet, Bernie told me that they send dead bodies by train in India. After that we saw quite a few, my son would say loudly *"another dead one"* What an education he was having!

We went to Agra to see the Taj Mahal, which is truly beautiful. But the town of Agra is certainly not, it's a very run down dirty little town with lots of" Herbies" running through the town seeing to the "sanitation," which is an open one there. I believe it's there my son got the food poisoning. Although we were as careful as we could be. We had gone to Jaipur for a few days before going back to Bombay when he started to get sick. He couldn't hold anything down. I was very worried and one morning I thought I'd take him for a walk to revive him a bit. As we passed a market, I saw what looked to be a doctor sitting at a table outside a stall. But he was smoking which was strange. There was a glass with water and a tonometer in it. A strange surgery, but there's a lot of strange things in India. He beckoned me to come over I did hold my son's hand. I explained the sickness to him, He then shocked me my nodding his head from side to side saying," *Malaria*". He wrapped up some big coloured tablets in newspaper, which looked like marbles and charged me a few rupees. I came away in an awful sate, rushing back to the hostel where we were staying, and told the receptionist. She laughed and said take no notice of a market doctor, there's a doctor next door who used to be part of the British Airforce. He came to us, much to my relief and said its food poisoning and gave my son an injection of antibiotics, much to his disgust. He promised to come every till my son was better, but I had to tell Philip he wasn't coming again. After a few days I knew he was on the mend, when he hid under the bed and had to be prised out, shouting" *get drunk and go home*". I had to hold my hand over his mouth! He used to see the Doctor and say" *Mom it's that bad man again*".

We reached the airport in one piece, if a little underweight due mostly to diaria. We longed for normal plain food as we waited for the plane, we talked of all the food we would have, roast lamb, mashed potatoes. Our mouths were watering at the thought.

What can I say about India, it makes me mad, and glad, and sad, and shocked, but never indifferent, and it's a marvellous, wonderful, horrific place which I'm glad to have visited.

The Town Hall

"*Dong Dong Dong*", went the town hall clock, loudly, a bit too loud for Sargent Harold Hayward, who was sauntering along right under the town hall. Clock, *"Dong bloody dong"*, he said a little too loudly as a passer-by stared at him. He quickened his pace, with an embarrassed sigh and followed the road along the promenade, the church clock still peeling away. It wasn't that clock in periarticular that annoyed him so much but it seemed to him as if there was, constant bells ringing for masses or funerals. The whole truth of it was if he admitted it to himself was, he didn't like Ireland. Although when he had heard of the posting he was elated. Well after all, the Somme where he had fought in trenches of mud it seemed like paradise. It still gave him nightmares, the stench of decaying bodies and the smell of trench foot, seeing a dead friend pinned to the wire of the trench in front of you and being unable to move him in case a bullet hit you too. So really, he shouldn't complain but he really wasn't prepared for the complex political situation here. You didn't know your enemy, you could be shot by a nationalist at any time, they used guerrilla warfare tactics here, and you always had to be on guard. Although some of the Irish were fine, and bore you no grudge. After all he had fought alongside of them in the trenches, but then there was a common enemy," Gerry." He wished he'd been schooled in a bit more history to understand it better, but he was only a common soldier.

He had reached the *"Peoples Park"* by this time "people's park, he thought how silly is that what else would a park be for animals?" he thought with distain. He sat down near the fountain on a bench where an elderly man also sat. He looked up at the sky it was grey, the elderly man said *"lovely day"*. Harry agreed but thought to himself *"the Irish had a funny sense of what a lovely day was.* But he supposed as long as it didn't rain, they were happy as it rained here,.....A Lot! He suddenly remembered that tonight was the night of the town hall dance. "" *Bloody ell* "that's all he needed to add to his gloomy mood. But he'd promised his buddies he go along. Sighing he got up to go back and change for it. He would go the the mess first for a few pints of real English ale, It might help to lift his mood a little.

Siting in the mess he felt a little better, a few guys were playing pool and their cheery cockney chatter reached his ears. *"No mate it's your round"* the tall blond guy was saying laughing to his friend. The banter cheered him a little, but looking down at his fast-disappearing beer, he realised that the beer was playing a role in it too.

When Harry and his two friends, Mac and Chris reached the town hall, the bell was pealing out eight. Dong dong. Harry addressing his friends said" *donging away as usual"*, Mac laughed at the remark. They entered the tall ballroom, which was gaily lit up for the dance. A band were playing *"Blue Moon".* Couples circled the dance floor waltzing to the music. It was then he saw her. He thought he'd never seen such a beautiful girl. She waltzed by them in the arms of a very tall man which made her look even smaller than she was. She wore her blond hair up, in the style of the day and green diamond earrings glittered in her ears. But what hit Harry most was her happy face; she looked like she owned the dance and was singing along to *Blue Moon* like she was the happiest woman alive. Harry thought she looked like a little beautiful bird. He followed her with his eyes, hoping that she wasn't involved with the tall man. The dance ended and the band started to play, a Glen Millar number. He was relieved to see the tall man dance by with someone else, so he walked round looking for her. Suddenly he noticed a drinks bar and she stood there waiting. Usually Harry was quite shy, but he was so dazzled by her he walked straight up to her and asked her to dance. She smiled and nodded and they joined the other couples on the dance floor.

They danced together all night and talked like they had known each from another life. She sang along to all the dance numbers, she seemed to know all the words, she told Harry she loved to sing and dance. He said "in *going to call you Birdie from now on*". It was midnight as they left the town hall the clock went its usual *dong dong*, Harry said to Birdie" *I love that sound, don't You*? Harry didn't know it then but he would be hearing that sound for the rest of his life. He would settle here and have ten children and even say on a grey day *"lovely day"* I know this as I am the granddaughter. I love to walk by the town hall and image the night they met there as the town hall clock goes, *"Dong dong dong"*

Winnie

The street was a very nice street with well-kept gardens roses growing round the doors. I moved there with my young 3-year-old son in 1987. The neighbours were friendly, Nell and her husband next door and Winnie upstairs with her husband. Although I felt distanced from them as I was alone. Winnie was the friendlier, she spoke excellent English. She was a sales lady as opposed to just a shop assistant. Those old-fashioned sales ladies in black who are well made up in the more affluent shops.

I often saw her arm in arm with her husband going out in the evenings looking very happy. She loved children even the ones I considered brats. She loved them all and gave them sweets maybe it was because she didn't have children herself.

Some years after I moved in Winnie's husband died and a year after that Nell's husband also died. I began to think I'd put a spell on the street. WE all got along very well the three of us and chatted on the long summer evenings although they were some 20 years older than I Sometimes I invited them for a glass of wine in my garden. They were happy days.

Winnie had a big party on her seventh birthday and wanted me to sing with her on the occasion. We practiced singing together By Bye blackbird. ON the night we all travelled to the event. I sang the song with Winnie much to my son's embarrassment.

It began very slowly, the senile dementia that Winnie had fallen victim of. She would pop her head out the window when I was going to work and ask what day it was. She had since retired although she had always been a very well-kept woman, she now started to look unkempt with food-stained clothes. About this time, she started to wear an old beige raincoat and strange hat. She looked like a bag lady so unlike her former self. She also adopted a stray cat and called him after the street Drebble. She became a very familiar sight calling for her cat in her long trench coat.

One Day I found her in my garden picking up stones I had put stones in the garden in place of grass She asked could she have them I said of course She said there were faces on them but I failed to see them. I used to do Winnie's hair for her at that time, one day she seemed very agitated she told me that husband had been an awful man. I told her to visualise him in the flames of hell. This seemed to make her happy, I asked Nell about her husband and Nell said it's the dementia as they had got along fine and he was a nice man. Soon after that big bald patches appeared on my front garden from the missing stones. Nell feared the ceiling would fall on top of her from all the stones Winnie's flat became a shrine to stones they were in buckets and bowls and along every surface. She said to me I just love stones, don't you? Mm I replied. We discussed what to do about her but didn't really know if we could interfere. She had nieces but I had never seen them calling.

What was to happen I was party instrumental in bring the attention to her niece but I didn't know it then. It happened one Sunday night at about ten. Winnie knocked on the door rather distraught. There was blood on her legs. My son said if you clean the blood off, I'll take her to hospital looking very squeamish, No I'll take her I said as he needed to study. I cleaned her up as much as I could and we went by taxi to the And E. They put us in a tiny cubicle and started to ask Winnie questions. When asked her age she said to me Margaret how old is I. I tried to think back to her seventh birthday and told them about 77. They finally discharged her at 3 am telling her to reach her GP in the morning. When we reached the street Winnie wanted to go look for her cat. I left her to it I had done enough of the Samaritan for one night.

Next day I knocked at her door to ask had she rang her doctor. She looked at me blankly and said Doctor. I said we were in the hospital last night. She replied we were why. I realised she had no memory of it. I knocked at Nell's door who said she would get in touch with her niece.

After those things happened very quickly. Her niece took her to the doctor and it seemed she had bowel cancer as well as dementia. How sad. Dementia doesn't discriminate it goes to people from all walks of life. Winnie had been such an accomplished person who could sing and play the piano. It was decided to send her to a hospice: but she didn't need to go as she died the night before her admission.

Nell and I and my son went to the crematorium together. There was a beautiful photo on top of the coffin of Winnie looking radiant just like she used to be. The niece said lovely things about her aunt. Nell and I looked at each other when she talked about her favourite Aunt. Wondering where she had been. She said there something Winnie would like you all to have to remember her by and as we walked out, we were all given a stone. What a lovely gesture, although the stones were mine really.

WE all had a glass of wine at the reception after. Nell said to me when I die, I'm not having people having drinks at my expense. I made a mental note not to go to Nell's funeral.

Soon after Nell moved, and after that I moved as well I've been to the street a few times it doesn't look well-kept as it used to. The gardens are unkempt and Nell's roses are gone. But in my mind's eye I can see the ghost of Winnie picking up stones and calling Drebbel and Nell pruning her ro.

The Wife of Bath

I left school in 1967, when dinosaurs still roamed around. Although I was happy enough with jobs such as waitress shop-assistant, home help, I always wondered how I would have done had I had an education, as I was an avid reader and had an intense need to know more. I travelled to London Jersey and Holland, but finally came home to Ireland. I began my adult education at age 60! I did my Junior and leaving certificate and then followed a creative writing course and had some short stories published. I was accepted in the Open-Learning programme at UCD, and had enough points to start a degree in Literature and History.

The big day in 2017 arrived, I stood in Campus wanting to bury myself or at least wear a paper bag over my head. I hid my middle-aged self behind a tree. I had imposter syndrome. What was I doing here with these bright young people? Their youth shining through, with long hair, some streaked with blue and purple, wearing jeans with holes in the knees. They had the world at their feet, my feet had trodden another path, the path of life, and they had a few bunions. I heard their conversation "Wow that's so not amazing" I'm so not ready for this". I finally crept from behind the tree, and thought about cutting some holes in the knees of my jeans, or perhaps a blue streak in my hair? I finally entered the lecture hall, and hid behind a pole at the back. Although I was mesmerised at the lecture and so happy finally to be in college, I still had a feeling of not belonging.

As time went by I noticed in tutorials that these young people were not as confident as they appeared. They blushed and were reluctant to speak. I didn't blush at all and loved to ask questions. My mind seemed to have no bounds or limits to the knowledge I was soaking up. I often thought of my life as a home help in Holland to older people. I thought of the hoovering I had done for them. Probably miles of carpet! Now my mind was being stimulated with all this. I would sit in the lecture hall listening to Dermot Ferreter, feeling such elation at my changed life.

Everything changed about my feeling of not belonging however in an English Literature class. We were studying Chaucer's, "Wife of Bath "and the tutor wanted us to put the story in a modern context, it was a contest with all the literature students She chose teams of students to work on this. It was a great experience, I really got to know these younger students in my team. We had to meet quite often to work on this project. It was great fun, I simply got into the spirit of the thing, I was just one of the guys. We decided to do a radio podcast of "The wife of Bath "with a presenter interviewing the various characters. I played the nun who berates the wife as a scarlet woman. I mimicked her voice in a Margaret Thatcher arrogant and judgemental voice condemning the "Wife of Bath" We were nominated for winning the contest but didn't win, but we got a mention. As I sat in the lecture hall with my now, buddies, I felt an enormous amount of camaraderie. After that I joined the student at coffee breaks and outside of campus. I joined them if they sat on a bus I was on. I felt, I really belonged thanks to "The Wife of Bath"! In fact, I probably always did, ageism is sometimes in our own head, our own insecurity. I overcame that feeling of not belonging in UCD. My four years in UCD were the most revealing years of my life.

I was so happy there, not only did I achieve my degree, I learned a lot about myself and others. I had thought I was mature, but I wasn't, I grew up there. I lost my insecurity, I gained confidence as well as knowledge. I continue to take courses through UCD Lifelong Learning. Those four years were some of the happiest of my life, oh and by the way I never did cut the holes in my jeans or put a purple streak in my hair. I didn't need to; I knew I belonged there anyway.

A Grave Affaire

A recent chest infection I had, and was put on steroids to kill the infection, led me to think back to being a home help in Holland and witnessing all kinds of ailments and illness. I was working for this man who was so ill with COPD he was permanently on steroids. Which is a wonder drug, but has radical side effects like shedding of skin, where skin becomes so paper-thin it flakes off like snow all the time. This job is not for the faint-hearted!

I was quickly briefed by the office before I went for the first time, that Jan Jansens wife had cancer and as she was his carer could no longer look after him due to her own illness. "Oh no I thought this is going to be difficult to handle" but you do the job that you were trained to do. Three months training in psychology and how to deal with people who are ill. But all we learned is theory, and reality is somewhat different. Knocking at a door for the first time is nerve raking, as you never know who you're going to get. You then had to prove yourself to the client as they did to you, both parties were watchful in the first few visits. If you proved yourself, i.e., that you were not going to run off with the family jewels or put the cat in the microwave then you were welcomed and you established that the client was not likely to lock you up in the cupboard as a slave, then you could establish a working relationship. The man who opened the door was a big man, a thin tube was in his nose leading to small oxygen bottle at his side, he was well dressed in a shirt but the flaking skin was noticeable. I was soon to find out the serious nature of lung diseases spotted a wheelchair in the corner. He walked me into a very clean and pleasant house. As he walked his breathing was laboured with the effort of walking. I met his wife who was very ill and in bed. I did the required chores and breathed a sigh of relief that the first day was over. The Jansens were only in their early sixties, to have such serious illnesses. This job made you so thankful for your own good health.

I never did get to know Mrs Jansen as a few weeks later I arrived at the house in the middle of a funeral! The office had failed to get the message to me! I apologised profusely (we were the front line of this organisation) Mrs Jansen had passed away but the home help was unaware of this due to the lax office staff, who never have to deal face to face with the client!

So began Mr Jansens grieving period, this is where people skills are put to the test, (in Dutch mensen kennis) In the beginning he was very sad, which is only natural. I would catch him looking at the many photos in frames of her and him together on the shelf and dusted by me. He would have tears in his eyes. But he had sons and a daughter to support him and I did what I could as well, trying to be empathetic as I could be. But as the year went by, he seemed to get slightly better, but not in his health. The continuing shedding of flakes of skin which I found everywhere, and his wheezing remained. He was a clever man who was a whizz in computers, where he spent a lot of time on. We got close during this time, like father daughter. We chatted during coffee breaks and he was good company. He once asked me why I didn't have a Dutch passport as I had been there over 20 years and could apply for one. The Dutch character is a practical one, not the Irish spiritual dreamy character, with all of its history on your shoulders. I said it was too hard fought for to give up, many have died to have this document to our freedom. Of course, he didn't understand.

Now, comes the interesting part, Mr Jansen went to his wife's grave every week with flowers. He was as mobile as he could be and installed himself in his car with his oxygen beside him and drove there. When he came back from the graveyard, he told me he had met an old girlfriend of his who was visiting her husband's grave, they had gone for coffee afterward! Graveyards romance, that's where it's all happening! I was quite amused at this meeting, as he seemed lighter in himself. It then became a regular occurrence. But one day he was agitated and told me she wanted it to go further? I laughed out loud, when he said how can I even cuddle her I can't dry myself with a towel after a shower, I sit in a towelling dressing gown until I'm dry. However, they must have solved the problem as the graveyard romance went on. Then it blossomed out of the graveyard, and in to having coffee at the house. I met her but wasn't too sure about her motives, and noticed a distinct coolness on his daughter's face. She was a lot healthier than he. He however was also blossoming and seemed to be on top of the world and surprisingly became more agile. All you need is love it seems. She moved in with him then. I went to dust the frames with his wife and him in them and they were gone! I asked him where they had gone and he replied Slyvia did not want to look at dead people!

As time went on Mr Jansen became more demanding of me, which he never had been before, asking for more tasks to be done. I realised this was sylvia influence, I no longer liked going there anymore, and dragged my feet every week. Then the surprise of surprises, he told me they were getting married. I was glad he was happy, but wondered at her motives, as he had a beautiful house and was quite comfortable. He then asked me to be there on the day to help with coffee as he knew I had waitress skills! I thought why not it's my day there it will be easier than chores. But on the other hand, he was using me as a waitress! No, it was not easier than chores. People kept nodding to me for coffee and cake, I felt like a servant. Plus, I knew the office would not approve, that's what I got for breaking rules! At last, the day was over. Footsore and weary I cycled home, having said my goodbye to the beaming happy couple.

Then what happened as a result of them getting married, the rate of money he had to pay was doubled and they decided not to have help ant more. Although I told him I was sad to go I wasn't really. I had been happy for the 2 years before the graveyard romance. I was so happy to leave and go elsewhere. Sometime later I went to a woman to help just for a day, as I was dusting, I found the very same photo frame with Mr and Mrs Jansen! I asked her and told her I had been the help there. She was the sister of Mrs Jansen it's a small world. She spoke about her family's disgust at how quickly Jan had got over her sister's death and how besotted he was with Sylvia, he did whatever she wanted, and all the changes he had made that wiped away his wife's memory If there is a moral to this story, what is it? That you're never too old or too sick for love. And love can be found everywhere even in a graveyard.

Queen of Supplements

I have an addiction. Yes, my name is Margaret and I'm a vitaholic. Supplements are my chosen drug. That's a plus, as you don't have to hide it. It takes time and effort, to deal with this addiction. Hours of looking up health issues on the net. Whatever ailment I have, or friends have, I'm on my laptop finding "cures" for it, resolving it. Consequently, I take up to 15 supplements a day. I line the little darlings up and smile. My "live forever" stash, I take first my lemon water (cleanses the liver, squeaky clean} Together with the vitamins for the liver, I feel I can have my few beers in the evening, as the following day it will again be washed clean, a bit like a car wash! Let me bring you through the vitamins and their benefits. You can sing along with it if you like.

A. is for the eye-sight so far as we can see. B is for the blood we need, running round with glee. **C.** is for immunity, for germs from the community. **D.** is for bones and teeth, a must if we want to eat. **E.** is for the skin in which were covered, hides wrinkles too if you're bothered. **F.** is for the omega, not the watch, but oil, which we need. **G.** has another name riboflavin, so not to confuse. **H.** is for the energy that we daily use. **I.** is for the iron for energy and zest. J. is for the use of brain, so put it to the test. **K.** is like a lorry, delivers calcium to bones. **L.** is for the mood, tends to make you bright. **M.** is important to relax the heart muscle. **N.** is for niacin, for the gut, to insure no bustle. **O.** again is omega oil looks after the heart, beating with no fuss. **P** has another name, Flavonoids, antioxidant, fights with all its might. **Q 10** is another fighter; insures you live forever. **R.** again feeds the brain, keeping it altogether. **S.** is for the balance of all. **T.** is for thymine, for those who drink and a good pal- a-mine. Last of all is **Zink**, also good, if you like a drink.

So that's my little army of helpers. Battling every day to keep me above the ground, not under it and I must say, as I'm now 71 and in reasonable health. Osteoarthritis, but K looks after that. A few gut problems but probiotics are helping there. Alcohol a little high in blood tests, milk thistle '/looking after that. All in all, not doing too bad. So Vitaholic is the new label. Everyone seems to have a label nowadays, so why not me. Although I don't like these labels. Why can't you, if you feel a bit hyper, like you just say I'm having an ADHD day or if you clean the house say I'm a bit OCD today. Or if your annoyed say I'm a bit phycho today. I think we're all a bit of everything to some extent or other.

Where does all this come from, I wonder? Shrinks tell us it all goes back to childhood? Funny enough I have a brother who takes a lot of supplements as well, he also goes to the gym and runs every day, well I have to admit I do online Zumba. Coincidence? Well on a more serious note, our family seem to just pop their clogs and go, No doctors or warnings. You're left with a feeling of where are they. The shock is enormous. We lost our father at 47, we were only in our 20s, it took years to come to terms with it. Then we lost the youngest brother, he was just 43. So, analysing it I would say, those two shock deaths had such a profound effect on us. It could explain the addiction to supplements. Anyway, must go now time for my online Zumba class.

The Flask People

Some years ago, having read *"Angelas Ashes, by Frank Mac Court,"* which I greatly enjoyed. What I loved in particular was the humour he applied, to the misery of an Irish Childhood. His book was set in Limerick; I think late thirty's. What struck me was although my childhood was fifties and sixty's Dublin, I could still resonate with a lot of what he wrote about, some twenty years later. The misery of the Irish Childhood, still existed, in fifties and sixty's Maybe when you don't have money, humour is the only way to get through.

I was born in 1953, in a country, although had existed since ancient times, had only some thirty years earlier been born. A baby crawling so to speak. Poverty and unemployment were rife. We had yet to court the Yankee dollar, but we were learning quickly, to become, the wealthy multi-racial land we know today. I regress, back to Dublin in the fifty's when the first baby steps were taken. The Church then had great power; it seemed to rule every aspect of Irish life. People respected it, or to be honest were frightened of it. Nuns taught in schools, and were nurses in hospitals, they held the reins and were the main body. If you were in hospital the wards were full of religious paintings on the walls. Bleeding pictures of Jesus looked down installing guilt into you. Ghostly nuns, with rosary beads rattling, wafted through the corridors, and the rosary was mandatory every night in the wards. I think you get the picture; sin was everywhere we were told. Sins and sins and more sins and even occasions of sin. Guilt was another weapon that was used to indoctrinate us. Guilt for being born, for sinning before we were born, guilt for being poor, that was a big sin then.

We walked to school about two miles away, my mother only had a penny each for us, as four were school-going. We had a choice to bus there or back. We were always late, so we took the bus in the morning and walked home. We walked the posh way home, through the wealthy area, where there were orchards with great pickings of apples and pears. If you were late, the nun would be standing at the door with a large round stick. That soon warmed your poor cold hands! There was a large hut in the school yard, it was where we poor kids went for our free milk and sandwich for lunch. The well-off kids were allowed to stay in the class room, with their fancy no crusts sarnies and flask of tea. There was a woman in a Pinney called Mrs Jenkins, who oversaw the operation. She too had a stick, in fact, they all seemed to have sticks then, to chastise us. We walked in the hut where crates of milk awaited us. We each took a small bottle and had to drink it as we slowly walked around to the large crate of sandwiches. All under the beady eyes of Mrs Jenkins, yielding her stick in case we just drank the cream on top. It took great skill to do that, and put the bottle slyly back with the watery milk with ice back in the crate. Then we got our sandwich, and back out to the yard, hail rain, and snow. We were the poor, and not allowed back in the classroom with the well-off kids. I was slowly beginning to see the class structure then at a very young age. Do you get the picture: poor are guilty of being poor! The sandwich fillings were, I can still remember:

Monday Cheese,

Tuesday Brawn (which we all hated)

Wednesday bun,

Thursday brawn (Again!)

Friday Jam

Tuesdays and Thursday's brawn days were misery days, as we stood in the cold and rain, the trick was to remove the brawn and drop in on the ground without catching the eye of a passing nun. After returning to class, the head nun would come to all the classes with a plate of the discarded brawn. The lecture would begin, how ungrateful we were, how people in Africa would be grateful to have this free meal. Guilt again, heaped on us, sins and guilt, guilt and sins.

I decided one year I was going to join the flask people and be nice and warm in the classroom, I would ask for a flask at Christmas. The big day arrived I got my flask. In those days there was no euro or cheap shops so a flask was an expensive item. I proudly walked to school with my flask in my schoolbag delighted with myself, I was a notch up on the pecking order, I felt taller now I was a flask person. At lunchtime I sat in the class proudly opening my flask of tea, watching my poor pals going out in the snow for their free lunch.

Sadly a few weeks later I dropped it and it broke, so back to the hut for the cold milk and brawn sandwich to eat in the rain. My very own Irish Catholic childhood memory.

I love the country we have become, although its taken 100 years to get here. It's been a very painful journey, with the Ryan report on child abuse. The church lost its power over the people of Ireland with all the accusations. Gone are the sins and guilt installed in us. Schools have lay teachers and there are no longer nuns in the hospitals, also gone are the pictures of bleeding effigies. The standard of living has improved greatly, although we still have problems. I love to see the young confident Irish people, who seem guilt and sin free. It puts me in mind of the song *"And the young People walking down Grafton Street, and everyone looking so well, I remember that Summer in Dublin"* Ireland was a baby crawling in the 50s, now that baby has taken its first steps of walking.

A short one act play

Two Dublin Men in a Garden during Corona Virus.

Setting; a wooden fence lies between the two men. It is a Spring Day with birds singing, and the second week of lock-down. Joe sits on a garden chair, and shouts *"Ed arye der?"*

Sound of door opening, and Ed sits on chair at the other side of the fence, saying *"Shoosh, don't want her indoors to hear. Gimme a can,"* Joe passes one through the slats to Ed.

Sound of can opening, "ta Joe gorgeous" and asks *"howja doing with dis social distancing?"" Grand* replies Joe, *I was never a one for too much distance anyway, always kept me distance."*

Joe: *"Jayses, me heart is in me mouth when I go to the supermarket, I keep thinking there's going to be no beer, dey can keep their toilet rolls as long as dey leave the beer!"*

Ed; *"too right, Joe, but the missus is worried bout me enlarged liver, and watching me like a hawk"*

Joe: *"Did dey say how enlarged it was".*

Ed: *"Never thought of asking"*

Joe: *"There will be many a few with enlarged livers be the time dis is over; sure, arnt the mothers all going mad trying to teach the kids at home. Id say thed be taking a fair ould drop, wouldn't you? Image how those kids will turn out being schooled by drunken parents?"*

Ed;" *laughing, it's like World War two isn't it Joe"*

Joe; *"No its worse, at least they all were together in the bomb shelters having a sing song"*

Ed; winking, *"Yeah n I heard the girls wer all very willing as well, wha Joe"*

Joe: *"At least ye knew de enemy, wha"*

Ed; *"yeah, ye can't see dis Corona ting"*

Joe: *"Cud be anywhere, dats de problem"*

Ed: *"Diya miss de pub, Joe?"*

Joe;" *I do an I don't, ya know, sitting on an ouwl stool with a load of ouwl cronies".*

Ed; *"Yer rite ya know, here we are having a can in the yard with da birds singing, helping our country".*

Joe: *"Ye an ye know were saving the country doing it, as Leo Verruca told us wha"*

Ed; *"Hes yer man allrigh, isn't he a doctor anyway?"*

Joe: passing a can through for Ed, and burping loudly" As the fella sez Ed, *"better six feet apart than six feet under "*

Ed*:" Dats rig*h, opening the can saying, *cheers Joe"*

Joe;" *Wha diya think of yer man O Houlihan de medical guy?"*

Ed*;" Id say hes a sound guy, wha, one of the lads."*

Joe: *"I'd say hed be a man who would like a drink, a man's man, not like Verruca, hed be having a glass of wine with the girls wha,"* laughing.

Ed; taking a swig of beer saying," *yer righ a man's man like us righ, Joe."*

Sound of door being opened, and a shrill woman's voice is heard, *"Edward, hope you are not drinking you know wha de doctor said"*

Ed; pushing beer cans through the fence replies," *no love just coming in now, bye Joe"*

Joe; signing,*" man's man allrigh, he's more scared of his wife than the Corona virus"*

A Tribute To Dublin

Dublin, we salute you, on this memorable date.
City of great charm, of things past and great.
Although no longer, youngster, but woman worldly wise.
You still show a sparkle, beneath the disguise´

Dublin, you show a wrinkle, more of humour than of age.
A history, full and splendid, written on every page.
You've seen a tear or two, on that fatal day of old.
When your streets, ran red, with youngster's brave and bold.

As I walk your streets, I fancy, I hear
The ghost of Molly's barrow, somewhere, still near.
As I stroll along the Liffey, I can almost hear the voice,
Of Behan, of Oscar Wild, not forgetting Joyce.

In its cosy bars, her children, can tell a tale or two.
With a wit, that's only unique to you
A city that's merged old and new,
Dublin, I take a bow to you.

From Moore Street to the Coombe, Dun Laoghaire on the coast,
Dubliners one and all raise to you a toast.
To a thousand years of laughter, poetry and folklore.
Dublin, you produced them all and more.

OH Dublin, lovely lady, with Pogues, Geldof, and Drew,
We raise a glass to greet you, and say,
Dublin, here's to you.

Printed in Dunstable, United Kingdom